D0577480

in
the
news™

DOMESTIC SPYING AND WIRETAPPING

Brad Lockwood

ROSEN
PUBLISHING®

New York

For the Fourth Estate: keeping the press free, government honest, and America democratic

Published in 2007 by The Rosen Publishing Group, Inc.
29 East 21st Street, New York, NY 10010

Library of Congress Cataloging-in-Publication Data

Lockwood, Brad.
Domestic spying and wiretapping / Brad Lockwood.—1st ed.
    p. cm.—(In the news)
Includes index.
ISBN-13: 978-1-4042-0973-2
ISBN-10: 1-4042-0973-5 (library binding)
1. Intelligence service—United States—Juvenile literature.
2. Espionage—United States—Juvenile literature. 3. Wiretapping—United States—Juvenile literature. I. Title.
JK468.I6L568 2007
363.325'1630973—dc22

2006024438

Manufactured in the United States of America

On the cover: Clockwise from top left: Devices and parts used to tap into phone lines; Michael Killeen (holding sign) and others protesting in Chicago, Illinois, against National Security Agency (NSA) wiretapping policies in 2006; and U.S. Attorney General Alberto Gonzales testifying on executive powers during wartime at a Senate Judiciary Committee hearing on Capitol Hill, February 6, 2006, in Washington, D.C.

contents

Balancing Power in the Age of Terrorism

Ever since America was a colony of England, concerns about individual privacy and speech, as well as limits on any government's ability to search and seize property, have remained forefront. Equally important is the effectiveness of presidential powers, ultimately broadened during times of war or other conflicts.

Preserving Constitutional rights while also protecting the nation is a difficult balance to achieve. This balance between presidential and Constitutional power has been debated since the founding of the United States in 1776.

News reports in 2005 and 2006 revealed that President George W. Bush granted the National Security Agency (NSA) permission to eavesdrop on Americans after the 9/11 attacks. Once again, the issue of executive power versus Constitutional rights made headlines. When it was made public in 2005 that Americans' conversations and correspondences were being monitored, journalists, lawyers, and pundits began arguing for and against potential infringements of our Constitutional rights.

Privacy rights are inferred in the Constitution but not specified. The First, Fourth, Fifth, and Fourteenth Amendments support privacy.

Wartime Powers

At the core of the argument is the expansion of presidential powers versus the core rights and limitations set forth in the U.S. Constitution and the Bill of Rights (its first ten amendments). Most Americans view these rights and executive limitations as the foundation of American democracy. The First Amendment ensures every American citizen's right to freedom of speech and the press, while the Fourth Amendment guarantees protection against unreasonable search and seizure. The Founding Fathers were adamant that the new nation protect the rights of its citizens. But could they have envisioned the advances in technology and stakes set forth by the threat of terrorism?

George Washington, the first president of the United States, as well as the general who united American troops in their opposition to England, expressed his feelings about spying. He believed that the intelligence gathered from spying was necessary, as was the secrecy needed to make the activity effective. In a letter to Colonel Elias Dayton on July 26, 1777, Washington wrote, "The necessity of procuring good intelligence is apparent and need not be further urged. All that remains for me to add is that you keep the whole matter as secret as possible."

Spying, by definition, is a secret undertaking. Once word is out that one party is spying on another, the entire effort is undermined. Meanwhile, the debate over the actual meaning of the U.S. Constitution and the intentions of the Founding Fathers has been ongoing. By creating a balance of power between the three branches of government—the executive (presidential), legislative (congressional), and judicial (the Supreme Court)—the Founding Fathers wanted no single person or institution to have absolute power. To guard against their fear of electing a tyrant like England's King George III, they designed the three branches to work together, establishing a system of checks and balances. While the

In this Currier and Ives lithograph, George Washington, commander of the Continental army, takes control of U.S. troops at Cambridge, Massachusetts, during the Revolutionary War on July 3, 1775.

president may set the policy for the country, Congress passes legislation and controls government spending, and the Supreme Court oversees and interprets laws, ensuring that the other branches abide by the Constitution.

Even though protecting the homeland is among the president's top priorities, history has shown that past leaders have abused their power. Former presidents Andrew Jackson, Woodrow Wilson, and Richard M. Nixon have each employed programs that conflicted with the system of checks and balances.

Starting with Washington, top-secret spying programs in particular have been endorsed by several former presidents, with and without the knowledge of Congress, the Supreme Court, or the public. There is only a debate of executive power and judgment when such programs are disclosed, opening the topic of domestic spying to the press, political parties, and the public. While the executive branch of government uses its power to protect Americans, Congress, the Supreme Court, the free press, and the public are left only to debate the impact and legality of such programs after they are already in place. While George W. Bush is not the first president to allow domestic spying, he probably won't be the last.

Intelligence Gathering After 9/11

What is drastically different from earlier domestic threats, however, is the impact of 9/11 on American foreign and domestic policies. Almost immediately after 9/11, the "War on Terror" was declared and led to an invasion first of Afghanistan and then of Iraq. In addition to these foreign policies, domestic policy decisions were also being made, though they were less noticed in comparison. The Bush administration put these programs,

Senator Patrick Leahy (D-Vermont) takes a photograph as President George W. Bush signs the Patriot Act in 2001. Others pictured are Senator Orrin Hatch (R-Utah, *far left*) and Senator Harry Reid (D-Nevada, *right*).

some of which were classified, in place. The most public was the passage of the USA Patriot Act. This legislation rewrote existing laws, reorganized intelligence agencies, and created the Department of Homeland Security—all with the goal of preventing future terrorist attacks on American soil. Also classified was President Bush's decision to authorize the NSA to eavesdrop on Americans' communications by telephone and e-mail, a program that wouldn't be made public for several years.

News about the new NSA policies was first disclosed in a *New York Times* article on December 16, 2005. In the article, James Risen reported that President Bush had issued an order in 2002 that allowed the NSA to monitor communications between Americans and those outside the United States. Reportedly focused solely on international communications, the reality that the NSA was suddenly spying on and wiretapping Americans was met with an uproar by the press and public. But it wasn't the legality of such spying that was in question—the NSA was allowed to perform such activities under existing laws—it was the president's decision to purposely defy those laws that put the entire program into question.

The Foreign Intelligence Surveillance Act

The Foreign Intelligence Surveillance Act (FISA), passed by Congress in 1978, permits federal wiretaps on American communications without the required warrants if intelligence officials can show "probable cause" that one of the persons communicating may be "an agent of a foreign power." FISA allows wiretapping, but it requires that officials apply for and receive the necessary warrants within seventy-two hours from a special FISA court. But the post 9/11-NSA program ignored FISA rules. Although President Bush and a select group of Constitutional lawyers and scholars endorsed the NSA program, breaking FISA is a felony punishable by five years in prison and a $10,000 fine.

Calls for an investigation into the NSA program were immediate, but so, too, were investigations into whom may have "leaked" this classified information to the press. Bush administration officials claimed that disclosing this secretive program was also illegal. The debate as old as our country was rekindled: How far can a president go to protect the American people?

America has always been split on issues that position the right to privacy against national security. In this case, President Bush defended the NSA program, congressional leaders took sides based on their party affiliation, and the public searched for answers.

It's an age-old debate: President Washington encouraged and actively participated in spying during the Revolutionary War (1775–1781). Abraham Lincoln suspended writs of habeas corpus (protecting a person or party from unlawful restraint and lengthy imprisonment without legal hearing) during the Civil War (1861–1865). Woodrow Wilson tapped the cables running across the Atlantic Ocean to get intelligence prior to and during World War I (1914–1918). Beginning in 1924, the director of the Federal Bureau of Investigation (FBI), J. Edgar Hoover, used domestic eavesdropping to build files (at times for blackmail) on hundreds of Americans under multiple presidents. And most famously, Richard M. Nixon illegally wiretapped and investigated, and even had burglarized, political opponents during the Watergate scandal of 1972. To show the varying degrees of opinions, Washington is still hailed as one of America's greatest presidents, as is Lincoln, who later went to Congress to gain approval for his wartime actions. However, Nixon was impeached and forced to resign in 1974 for his indiscretions.

Since 2005, calls for the impeachment—or at least congressional censure—of President Bush have been made, even as he continues to defend his actions. Congress, state courts, the Supreme Court, and the American public continue to debate the legality of the NSA. In this age of terrorism and technology, two questions can be asked: how far should a government go to protect the people and how many rights are people willing to sacrifice for their protection?

A Brief History of an Old Activity

Spying has been going on since the United States was founded. Gathering intelligence about an enemy's intentions and possible actions is invaluable during times of war.

During the Revolutionary War, for example, General George Washington used multiple spies to gain advantage over England, getting information on troop movements, and even giving incorrect information to foreign spies to deceive England. Historians agree that these clandestine activities played a major role in the victory at Yorktown and in allowing Washington's Continental army to evade English troops during winters at Valley Forge, and eventually winning America its independence. Afterward, Washington, then president, would continue to endorse spying, first asking for $40,000 to fund intelligence operations in 1790. By 1793, $1 million, or around 12 percent of the government's budget, was dedicated to such activities.

The spending on intelligence gathering has steadily grown, today reaching an astronomical $48 billion, as mistakenly disclosed (budgets for intelligence are normally classified) by John Negroponte, director of national intelligence, in 2006. Usually reporting directly to the president, various agencies have evolved into what is now known as the intelligence community. This is hardly an "open" community, however; competition within and among agencies exists with varied goals. It is generally accepted that the FBI is in charge of domestic matters; the Central Intelligence Agency (CIA), foreign matters; and the NSA, a wide range of confidential undertakings.

America's First Intelligence Agency

Even with these agencies, national security and individual rights sometimes suffer, and only at these moments does the public become aware of the capabilities and weaknesses of America's intelligence efforts. During the

War of 1812, for example, military intelligence failed to realize that British troops were within only 10 miles (16.1 kilometers) of Washington, D.C. During the Civil War, both southern Confederate troops and the northern Union troops ran spying programs, forcing President Abraham Lincoln to suspend habeas corpus, imprisoning suspected Southern sympathizers (and suspected spies) without prompt trials or legal council. In 1861, Lincoln also become the first president to use electronic transmissions of intelligence from balloons flying above battlefields and surrounding areas—advances in sharing information that later succeeded in detecting Confederate troops preparing to attack Virginia. By 1863, these successes led to the establishment of the first intelligence organization: the Bureau of Military Intelligence, which later became the Secret Service.

Future presidents would both embrace and scorn intelligence agencies. Theodore Roosevelt annexed the Panama Canal with the help of spies who incited a revolution in Panama. Then, in 1907, after learning of the Japanese military buildup through intelligence, Roosevelt launched a worldwide tour of the U.S. naval force, a public display of power that underscored his famous mantra, "Speak softly, but carry a big stick." President Woodrow Wilson was no fan of spies and was generally suspicious of intelligence gathered by their means, but World War I forced him to reconsider his stance. When

President Woodrow Wilson, speaking in 1917, entered his second term hoping to avoid World War I. By 1917, however, he convinced Congress to declare war against Germany.

British intelligence decrypted German communications showing that the Germans were trying to bring Mexico into the war against the United States, Wilson formed MI-8 in 1917. MI-8 was an intelligence agency formed to decode military communications by, among other techniques, the tapping of international communications carried over cables crossing the Atlantic Ocean. When the United States officially entered World War I that same year, it had already been gathering intelligence by spying and wiretapping. Afterward, Wilson's successor, Herbert Hoover, would return the nation to a climate of "anti-snooping." Hoover's Secretary of State Henry L. Stimson said in 1929, "Gentlemen do not read each other's mail."

Questionable Activities

J. Edgar Hoover (no relation to President Hoover), founder and director of the FBI, brought domestic spying to new heights in the 1930s and in the decades that followed.

Hoover helped sharpen FBI techniques and served under multiple presidents. Hoover's COINTELPRO program allowed FBI agents to tap phone calls and compile files on citizens (including civil rights leader Reverend Martin Luther King Jr. and Beatles singer/songwriter and activist John Lennon). Political opponents, viewed as threats to Hoover's position, were also targets, including brothers John F. and Robert F. Kennedy. People were haunted by the thought that the FBI had gathered information on them, potentially for blackmail purposes. But again, intelligence failures soon brought the agencies under criticism.

On December 7, 1941, the Japanese attacked Pearl Harbor, causing more than 2,400 deaths. Like 9/11, Pearl Harbor was an utter failure of intelligence. Disturbingly, no one knew that the Japanese were planning a surprise attack, bombing a fleet of U.S. Navy ships in Hawaii. Afterward, President Franklin D. Roosevelt demanded greater control over intelligence agencies. "Never again!" became the national outcry. Roosevelt established a centralized intelligence structure that started with the Office of Strategic Services (OSS) and the Military Intelligence Service (MIS) in 1942.

Subject to Reform

Intelligence agencies have constantly been invented, revised, erased, and then reinvented. Roosevelt's

President Franklin D. Roosevelt signs a declaration of war against Japan after the unexpected attack on Pearl Harbor, Hawaii, on December 7, 1941.

vice president and successor, Harry Truman, abolished the OSS in 1945 and created the National Security Council (NSC) and Central Intelligence Agency (CIA). The NSC was charged with coordinating civilian and military security, while the CIA would coordinate national security intelligence. Post World War II, the four existing agencies (MIS, NSC, CIA, and FBI) would be further bolstered by Truman's creation of the National Security Agency (NSA). Americans seemed to have domestic and foreign intelligence covered, but would the newly expanded system work? Within a decade, the United States had several intelligence agencies, each with its own authority. Their overlapping agendas, however, confused employees, Congress, and the public. Having one person in charge of all intelligence—titled DCI, or Director of Central Intelligence—was a position often filled but rarely useful. The agencies simply would not yield to one authority, including the president. It would take major scandals and the resignation of a president to again spark change and calls for oversight.

The Bay of Pigs and Watergate

The actions of intelligence agencies, when uncovered, had in the past seemed like the stuff of novels. Spies gaining valuable intelligence or giving misleading information to deceive enemies seemed more mysterious, almost romantic, than the strategies of war. The 1960s, however, brought the true cost of intelligence to the fore.

In 1961, President John F. Kennedy launched what became known as the Bay of Pigs invasion. Intent on overthrowing Cuba's Communist leader Fidel Castro, the CIA trained Cuban expatriates to invade Cuba with disastrous results. The U.S.-sponsored invasion was a failure; the CIA-trained invaders were routed, captured, or killed; and the American people were aghast. What was the CIA doing without our knowledge?

Calls for investigations of the CIA's actions, however immediate, were overshadowed by the Cuban missile crisis in 1962 (led by secret aerial surveillance) followed by American intervention in Vietnam. Once again, attempts to bring all intelligence activities under one authority were ineffective. By the 1970s, America was in the midst of a quagmire in Vietnam. With tens of thousands of troops dead, Congress finally stepped in to determine the costs and activities of all intelligence efforts. This action was remarkable: for nearly 200 years, intelligence programs had been ongoing without Congress's involvement.

Multiple presidents and assorted agencies had been spending tax dollars on these efforts for centuries, but the part of the government that pays the bills and represents the people—Congress—had rarely been involved.

Watergate changed everything. Richard Nixon's wiretapping of political opponents—even allowing a break-in at the offices of the Democratic Party in the Watergate Hotel in Washington, D.C.—showed Americans how out of control a president could become without checks on his power. Lacking effective and essential oversight from Congress and the courts, Nixon had broken the law. Moreover, it was disclosed that Nixon had actually approached the CIA to cover up the break-ins at the Watergate Hotel, but was refused. Facing impeachment, a dishonored Nixon was forced to resign. Public disgust and debate over presidential powers were at their apex. The press responded by reporting on other intelligence efforts, including attempts to assassinate foreign leaders and destabilize foreign governments.

New Restrictions

In response to increased press coverage about intelligence activities, including spying and disclosing J. Edgar Hoover's history of wiretapping Americans, Congress took action. Multiple commissions were created to study the intelligence community, leading to new laws limiting its activities. In 1975, President Gerald Ford restricted the CIA's domestic activities; placed a ban on opening mail, wiretaps, and the abuse of tax information; and reversed mandatory drug-testing policies of suspected persons by agencies. Still, Ford neither disclosed the intelligence budget, nor did he agree to a separate congressional oversight committee.

FISA and the Iran-Contra Affair

President Jimmy Carter replaced Ford in 1977 and the following year passed the Foreign Intelligence Surveillance Act. Acknowledging that the use of wiretaps was essential to gain intelligence, but that oversight was necessary, FISA allowed electronic surveillance but forced officials to retroactively apply for and obtain warrants from a special FISA court. Top secret and confidential, this surveillance has continued for years with a select group of judges who review and approve the spying on communications by the NSA. However controversial, these activities are legal as long as the FISA court eventually hears proof of why people were being wiretapped within seventy-two hours.

Although FISA brought oversight to intelligence activities, agencies continued to act with little regard to the law. This became clear during the administration of Ronald Reagan, when intelligence budgets were increased, personnel was expanded, and the Cold War was in full bloom. As a result, agencies were given greater latitude to gather both domestic and foreign intelligence.

The Iran-Contra affair soon eclipsed concerns about domestic spying and wiretapping. In 1986, representatives of the Reagan administration sold military arms and weapons parts to the government of Iran at inflated prices, and then used the profits to underwrite anti-Communist rebels, known as the Contras, in Nicaragua.

The sale of weapons to a publicly declared enemy of America was highly questionable and illegal. But the fact that the administration was also using intelligence agencies to fund the overthrow of a Latin American government was unacceptable. Officials from multiple agencies would be indicted, found guilty, and jailed. Reagan's vice president and successor, former CIA director George H. W. Bush, would later pardon six of those charged in the Iran-Contra Affair in 1992.

Secret Identities

Many of those employed in intelligence agencies operate in secrecy. They use aliases and work for false companies. This is essential for them to protect themselves, their families, and other agents. Revealing the identity of a spy can be fatal. This was evident in 1994, when thirty-year CIA employee Aldrich Ames was charged with spying for the Soviet Union. He and his wife pled guilty and were sent

Former president George H. W. Bush appears before the Senate Armed Services Committee in 1975 shortly after he received the nomination to become the director of the Central Intelligence Agency (CIA).

to prison. But having disclosed several of the CIA's spies, many were arrested, imprisoned, or executed by the Soviet Union. Ames's misdeeds had fatal consequences.

But what if an agent reveals his or her own identity? Because intelligence agencies like to maintain distance— known as "deniability"—from their covert agents, when a spy or employee leaks information to the press or reveals information to investigators, the very nature of their work becomes controversial. Russell Tice, for example, the whistleblower for the *New York Times* story about NSA operations, knew about the operations because he worked at the agency. His insights were critical in exposing the secret NSA program, but by talking to the press, he put his career, and possibly national security, at risk.

It seems that only when there is a scandal or failure do intelligence operations become public. Not since Nixon has a president been able to declare such sweeping powers. Nixon's disgraceful resignation chilled the presidents who followed, ushering in an era of greater scrutiny. More than thirty years later, U.S. intelligence was tested again, in what would become our greatest failure.

The events of 9/11 were the result of a massive failure of intelligence, as noted by then National Security Advisor Condoleeza Rice in her admission before Congress that President Bush's daily briefing, presented only weeks before 9/11, was head-lined "Bin Laden Determined to Strike in U.S."

9/11

The events of September 11, 2001, proved to the world that American intelligence had failed. Those catastrophic attacks that used commercial jets as weapons to destroy the World Trade Center in New York City and damage the Pentagon outside Washington, D.C., killed nearly 2,800 Americans. The public demanded to know how the government had failed to see such a premeditated and diabolical scheme. The events of 9/11 were the result of a massive failure of intelligence, as noted by then National Security Advisor Condoleeza Rice in her admission before Congress that President Bush's daily briefing, presented only weeks before 9/11, was headlined "Bin Laden Determined to Strike in U.S."

Intelligence agencies knew Osama bin Laden wanted to attack America and that the nineteen hijackers were living in the United States and actively planning attacks. The full story behind 9/11 may never be known. Only now are new reports of intelligence officials' warnings of the strike being planned in e-mails and memos to their superiors surfacing. Still, all eyes were on Washington, D.C., the president, and Congress to take immediate action. What could be done to prevent another 9/11?

President Bush and Congress acted quickly. In addition to invading Afghanistan and then Iraq (though the Iraqi government and its dictator, Saddam Hussein, had

Declassified and Approved
for Release, 10 April 2004

Bin Ladin Determined To Strike in US

Clandestine, foreign government, and media reports indicate Bin Ladin since 1997 has wanted to conduct terrorist attacks in the US. Bin Ladin implied in US television interviews in 1997 and 1998 that his followers would follow the example of World Trade Center bomber Ramzi Yousef and "bring the fighting to America."

After US missile strikes on his base in Afghanistan in 1998, Bin Ladin told followers he wanted to retaliate in Washington, according to a ▬▬▬▬▬ service.

An Egyptian Islamic Jihad (EIJ) operative told an▬▬▬ service at the same time that Bin Ladin was planning to exploit the operative's access to the US to mount a terrorist strike.

The millennium plotting in Canada in 1999 may have been part of Bin Ladin's first serious attempt to implement a terrorist strike in the US. Convicted plotter Ahmed Ressam has told the FBI that he conceived the idea to attack Los Angeles International Airport himself, but that Bin Ladin lieutenant Abu Zubaydah encouraged him and helped facilitate the operation. Ressam also said that in 1998 Abu Zubaydah was planning his own US attack.

Ressam says Bin Ladin was aware of the Los Angeles operation.

Although Bin Ladin has not succeeded, his attacks against the US Embassies in Kenya and Tanzania in 1998 demonstrate that he prepares operations years in advance and is not deterred by setbacks. Bin Ladin associates surveilled our Embassies in Nairobi and Dar es Salaam as early as 1993, and some members of the Nairobi cell planning the bombings were arrested and deported in 1997.

Al-Qa'ida members—including some who are US citizens—have resided in or traveled to the US for years, and the group apparently maintains a support structure that could aid attacks. Two al-Qa'ida members found guilty in the conspiracy to bomb our Embassies in East Africa were US citizens, and a senior EIJ member lived in California in the mid-1990s.

A clandestine source said in 1998 that a Bin Ladin cell in New York was recruiting Muslim-American youth for attacks.

We have not been able to corroborate some of the more sensational threat reporting, such as that from a ▬▬▬▬▬ service in 1998 saying that Bin Ladin wanted to hijack a US aircraft to gain the release of "Blind Shaykh" 'Umar 'Abd al-Rahman and other US-held extremists.

continued

For the President Only
6 August 2001

Declassified and Approved
for Release, 10 April 2004

Pictured is the controversial August 2001 memo to President Bush that stated bin Laden wanted to strike U.S. targets. It indicated that members of Al-Qaeda were living in America.

no ties to 9/11 or bin Laden), new legislation and classified programs were promptly authorized. In 2002, the Patriot Act brought the various intelligence agencies under one umbrella group, the Department of Homeland Security. It was placed under the supervision of a single person, Tom Ridge, who would officially head the department the following January.

The years following 9/11 also saw a flurry of legislation and military activity—so much so that classified and potentially unconstitutional programs were enacted. These stealth surveillance programs included mobile and landline telephone wiretapping, the monitoring of electronic communications and banking transactions, data mining and profiling, and the interception of postal mail.

Like events that followed Pearl Harbor, when Franklin D. Roosevelt actively encouraged spying and forcibly removed all Japanese immigrants and Japanese Americans to confined locations, 9/11 also raised suspicions about specific groups. Middle Eastern men, especially those who might have been in the country illegally, were suddenly targeted. The Bush administration began imprisoning suspected terrorists as "enemy combatants" at a military base in Guantanamo Bay, Cuba, with no access to lawyers. Bush's actions defied the rules of the Geneva Convention, a set of treaties that were established beginning in 1864 to set the international guidelines of warfare.

Privacy in the Age of Terror

Americans, eager for action, were also sacrificing individual rights. They were now subject to thorough screenings at airports to ensure national security. President Bush, meanwhile, was using the events of 9/11 to encourage broader executive powers. The pre-emptive invasion of Iraq is just one of many controversial decisions that show his administration's agenda to expand executive muscle. In addition, he has issued signing statements that defy legislation, and called for increased monitoring of citizens.

Bush never intended for Americans—and certainly not our enemies—to know the full extent of domestic surveillance, but the expanded range of the NSA's reach became fully known after the *New York Times* story was published in December 2005.

As further disclosed in news articles after the *New York Times*' story broke, at one time, the NSA could monitor 5,000 to 7,000 people communicating through phones and/or e-mail. Supposedly limited to overseas activities, this was actually just half of the NSA program—or half of a dialogue—because many of these conversations involved other Americans or foreigners overseas. Americans may have been willing to accept foreigners, especially potential terrorists, having their calls intercepted, but fellow Americans being spied upon? These activities went beyond the NSA's authority. Under the

FISA law of 1978, if any American citizen was to be wire-tapped, the authorities had to go to the special FISA court to get a warrant. But Bush's secret order to the NSA defied this law. No one, not even judges on the special court, would know of this spying and wiretapping program; oversight by Congress and the courts was being ignored.

Thousands of Americans have undoubtedly been spied upon since 2002. In addition, the FBI and CIA expanded their spying activities, both here and abroad. According to Senate Judiciary Committee hearings with FBI director Robert S. Mueller III in May 2006, the FBI alone had sought 9,200 national security letters to obtain secret wiretaps of 3,500 individuals in 2005. (To provide some context for this figure, from 1979 to 1995, the FISA court had issued about 500 warrants per year; but recently that number has increased—even without the NSA program under its authority—to 1,738 in 2004.) Secret warrants for wiretaps were nothing new, but these figures still pale in comparison to the NSA program, which can handle that many conversations at any given moment. One former NSA official, and source for the original *New York Times* story, Russell Tice, said in an 2006 interview with ABC News that a "number of Americans subject to eavesdropping by the NSA could be in the millions if the full range of secret NSA programs was used."

A 2004 survey by the U.S. General Accounting Office (GAO) found multiple government agencies initiating 199 data-mining projects containing more than 120 software programs to collect and analyze personal data and predict behavior, numbers that have surely expanded since.

Tice was among James Risen's sources for the breaking 2005 *New York Times* article on the NSA's surveillance activities, a story that the paper had suppressed for more than a year due to overwhelming pressure from the White House. Once the program was made public, however, Americans were outraged.

According to Tice, all a person had to do to fall under NSA scrutiny was to say the word "jihad" over the phone or type the word "bomb" or "Osama bin Laden" into an e-mail and click "Send." The technology behind

New York Times correspondent James Risen, pictured in Maryland in 2005, first reported that the government had been spying on Americans without prior court approval since 9/11.

the NSA's secret surveillance programs uses "digital vacuum" tools to instantaneously capture communications, then data-mining software programs filter that information for specific keywords or phrases. The GEOcell program

then finds the exact locations where the information originated, connecting to satellite imagery to pinpoint from
where the communications are being sent. "Network the-
ories" and algorithms (mathematical equations) are then
run to connect conversations and other correspondences,
creating lists of potential terrorists or other criminals.

Most likely in response to Bush's defying FISA rules,
Judge James Robertson, a veteran on the bench of the
FISA court, resigned in 2006. In Senate testimony in
March 2006, Judge Robertson said, "Seeking judicial
approval for government activities that implicate consti-
tutional protections is the American way."

The legal implications of Bush's NSA program are
massive. Beyond his own actions, illegal or debatable,
there are others who assisted in the program. Telecommunications companies were soon having class-action
lawsuits filed against them by customers. AT&T is known
to have installed equipment for the NSA in its call-routing
centers; this was kept confidential until a former AT&T
engineer blew the whistle on such activities, even providing installation blueprints. Other telecommunications
companies have also assisted the NSA, which shows how
spying and domestic wiretapping programs require the
involvement, questionable and/or illegal, of many parties. Ironically, by trying to catch terrorists and criminals
through the NSA program, many people have broken
the law and possibly become criminals themselves.

A Divisive Debate

3

In 2006, former White House counsel John Dean, in discussion with California Senator Barbara Boxer, said, "[President] Bush is the first president to admit to an impeachable offense," summing up one side of the domestic spying debate.

But Senate Majority Leader Bill Frist defended the program. "We are right now . . . in an unprecedented war, where we do have people who really want to take us down," Frist said.

There are solid arguments to each side of the debate. While it's true that America is at war, and all means must be used to win, is breaking the law and subsequently eroding the rights and privacy of Americans an appropriate cost?

Perhaps at greatest issue was the public deception utilized by the Bush administration to keep the NSA program secret between 2001 and 2005. The needs of wartime intelligence gathering were among the defenses President Bush used after the NSA program was made public, insisting that it was of a "very limited nature" and did not involve Americans' phones being wiretapped.

In Buffalo, New York, on April 20, 2004, President Bush said, "Now, by the way, any time you hear the United States government talking about wiretap, it requires—a wiretap requires a court order. Nothing has changed, by the way. When we're talking about chasing down terrorists, we're talking about getting a court order before we do so. It's important for our fellow citizens to understand, when you think Patriot Act, constitutional guarantees are in place when it comes to doing what is necessary to protect our homeland because we value the Constitution."

At best, these statements were inaccurate; at worse, they were intentionally misleading. At the time, Bush knew that he was allowing the NSA to wiretap Americans without seeking necessary warrants. The president had broken, or at least defied, the 1978 FISA act and ignored the FISA court that was created to review secret wiretaps. Given these transgressions, Democrats

Protesters rally in Buffalo, New York, on April 20, 2004, while President Bush participated in a public conversation about the Patriot Act where he said, "A wiretap requires a court order."

called for the NSA program to end, and possibly, for investigations into whether the president had broken the law.

Once the activities of the NSA were made public, people began making comparisons between President Bush's defiance of the law and Nixon and the Watergate scandal. On January 5, 2006, a letter was sent to Bush from the House of Representatives, signed by Michigan Congressman John Conyers Jr. and Ohio Congressman Dennis Kucinich. The letter demanded "any and all records" on the number of Americans' communications intercepted by the NSA program.

Although the Bush administration claimed the information being sought was confidential and it refused to acknowledge the existence of the NSA, allegations soon spread that wiretaps were also being used to spy on political opponents and members of the press.

CNN journalist Christiane Amanpour reports on the state of Iraq from the roof of the Marriott Hotel in Islamabad, Pakistan.

One startling accusation that continued to persist without closure was that the Bush administration had tapped the calls of Christiane Amanpour, chief international correspondent for CNN. A vocal critic of the administration's policies, as well as a U.S. citizen of Iranian descent, Amanpour is married to Jamie Rubin, who served as a key campaign advisor to John Kerry during his presidential run in 2004. Had the Bush administration used the NSA for political gain, perhaps to help it win re-election? The implications of a president wiretapping with no oversight are vast and troubling. Powerful members of the president's Republican Party, John McCain and Arlen Specter, also questioned the program's legality.

Even before the NSA program was disclosed, Bush had problems. On December 18, 2005, Congressman Conyers introduced a resolution into the House of Representatives to form a committee to investigate the administration and "to make recommendations regarding grounds for possible impeachment." Conyers' basis was the administration's "intent to go to war [with Iraq] before congressional authorization, [and the] manipulating of pre-war intelligence . . . ," but the timing, only two days after the NSA program was disclosed, should have made for interesting debate. With Republicans in control of both the Congress and White House, however, Conyers' resolution gained little traction. Specific to the NSA program, on March 12, 2006, Wisconsin senator Russell D. Feingold said he would introduce a measure to censure, or officially condemn, President Bush over illegal wiretapping. Republicans quelled this move as well.

Was it politics at play, or something greater? Trumping these calls for independent investigation and oversight seemed to be the very expansion of presidential power, especially during times of war when the president remains in charge of national security.

After 9/11, Congress authorized Bush to wage the "War on Terror," passing the Patriot Act to ease the gathering and sharing of intelligence. Congress had played its role, authorizing the president to go to war, but post-9/11 legislation was extremely far-reaching.

Troubling Ties

U.S. Attorney General Alberto Gonzales, who supports spying on Americans without a court order, holds the FISA Act on February 6, 2006, while testifying before the Senate Judiciary Committee.

Adding to the discrimination of the NSA program were later revelations that the U.S. Attorney General at the time, John Ashcroft, had balked at authorizing the wiretapping program in 2004, forcing it to be suspended for two weeks.

Further crippling the credibility of the Bush administration was the announcement that Alberto Gonzales, legal advisor to the president, was heavily involved in providing advice and precedents to support the NSA and would soon succeed Ashcroft as the attorney general. Due to his unwillingness to acknowledge the existence of the NSA, even under oath at congressional hearings, this further complicated the administration's defense because, as attorney general, Gonzales might have to order the creation of an independent panel to investigate his own actions.

Yet another conflict of interest would surface when General Michael V. Hayden, director of the NSA from 1999 to 2005, was picked by Bush in May 2006 to succeed Porter Goss as head of the CIA. Among those also expressing doubts about Hayden's ability to run the CIA were a growing number of Republicans, who had questions and concerns about the program.

Predictably, the NSA program became a campaign issue. Early in 2006, an election year for Congress, advertisements started to condemn the administration due to the NSA program, while others praised it. One of the first, run by Sean P. Maloney, a candidate seeking the Democratic nomination for attorney general of New York state, said, "George Bush is secretly tapping American phones without a court order. Under New York law, that's illegal and wrong." At the same time, most Republicans argue that the program is essential to safeguarding America's national security. Obviously, the debate regarding the legality of the NSA extends beyond the Constitution and the courts. It was now seen as problematic to even be remotely associated with the secret program, especially during an election year.

> *"George Bush is secretly tapping American phones without a court order. Under New York law, that's illegal and wrong."*

Challenging the Courts

4

As the debate about whether or not the NSA wiretapping program is necessary to protect our nation's security, evidence obtained from the program is already being used against alleged criminals.

Muslim cleric and Virginia resident Dr. Ali al-Timimi was convicted in 2005 and sentenced to life in prison for "inciting his Muslim followers to violence." But his conviction and ultimate fate are now in question because of how the U.S. government won the trial.

Circumstantial evidence presented during the trial,

including incriminating conversations that al-Timimi had with other suspected terrorists, may have been obtained through the NSA's spying and wiretapping program. This eavesdropping, which began on al-Timimi shortly after 9/11, was illegal, said his lawyer, Jonathan Turley, because the NSA had no warrant. Therefore, Turley argued, the entire case should be dismissed and the Muslim cleric should be freed.

Future Conflicts

This was the first ruling by a federal court that relied on information gained through the NSA program. The U.S. Court of Appeals for the Fourth Circuit on April 25, 2006, directed the

Ali al-Tamimi *(center)* leaves a courthouse in Alexandria, Virginia, on April 18, 2005, where he was convicted of exhorting Muslim followers to join the Taliban against U.S. troops in Afghanistan.

lower court in Alexandria, Virginia, to consider al-Timimi's statements that he had been illegally wiretapped. While not ruling on the merits of al-Timimi's assertions about the illegality of the NSA program, the move by the court was significant. It was a sign of future conflicts with the use of illegally obtained information.

The critical role the NSA has played in cases against suspected terrorists such as al-Timimi can neither be understated nor fully known. This is why suspicions about the program, as well as repeated denials that it exists, jeopardize cases.

This signals dilemmas for the Bush administration: dozens of trials have already been completed, and many more are pending, all using information obtained through the NSA. While the Justice Department did not oppose the court's move to address the eavesdropping question, tremors are being felt throughout government. The secret nature of the NSA presents the greatest challenge to winning trials and upholding verdicts. "Whenever we have the opportunity to set the record straight, we'll do so," said Justice Department spokesman Bryan Sierra in response to the decision regarding al-Timimi's appeal. However, this may be rather awkward, due to Attorney General Gonzales's deep involvement in creating and authorizing the NSA program. How can the attorney general lead investigations into questionable activities that he helped authorize?

Moreover, how many future trials and convictions will be jeopardized by the secrecy and unlawfulness of the NSA program? "The government would have to establish whether al-Timimi was intercepted under this, or any other undisclosed operation, and the court could have to [examine] the legality of the whole operation," said Turley. This is a very serious matter, not only involving the future of intelligence gathering, but also the U.S. Constitution and Bill of Rights.

Free Speech or Sedition?

In the case of al-Timimi, this examination involves not only the Fourth Amendment, but the Fifth and First as well. While the Fourth Amendment protects against searches and seizures without warrants, which many believe the NSA program infringes upon, the Fifth Amendment protects against self-incrimination. By using unwarranted wiretaps against al-Timimi during his trial, jurors heard him implicating himself. Then there's the First Amendment, protecting freedom of speech and of the press. As a cleric, why can't al-Timimi speak his mind? Old laws against sedition—of speaking ill of the government or inciting others against it—are already being debated. Doesn't al-Timimi have the right to speak freely and express his religious beliefs, even if he was allegedly rousing his followers to commit acts of violence against America?

The Justice Department saw the appellate decision as "largely procedural," but the implications are vast. "This is very good news for us, and we're eager to go back to Judge Brinkema to explore these troubling issues," affirmed Turley. Whatever precedent arises out of this complex case will also carry weight in future trials where the evidence was gathered without warrants.

Other Lawsuits

A class-action lawsuit against AT&T for abetting the NSA in wiretapping Americans without warrants is in jeopardy because the U.S. government is arguing that it must be dismissed on "grounds of States Secrets Privilege." Basically, this means that the court will be breaking the law by airing classified government information just to argue the case.

In yet another case, the al-Haramain Islamic Foundation sued the U.S. government on February 28, 2006, in federal court. Similar to al-Timimi's argument, the suit argued that conversations were being intercepted without warrants. In this instance, however, the government had made a major gaffe. According to a March 2, 2006, *Washington Post* article, an anonymous source said the government had mistakenly given NSA intercepts to the al-Haramain Islamic Foundation. In a trial involving suspected terrorism activities by the foundation, the government had mistakenly given proof that the NSA was wiretapping its conversations. Instead of suspicions like al-Timimi's, the al-Haramain Islamic Foundation had proof of being wiretapped without

Pictured is the al-Haramain Islamic Foundation office in Bossaso, Somalia, where the group was allegedly running a school, Internet café, and money-transfer business.

warrants. At the time of this writing, the evidence for the case remains sealed.

Legal precedents are building. How much longer can the NSA deny the existence of its program? How many more people will be tried based on evidence that they cannot review or even learn where it originated? Will people such as al-Timimi, an outspoken solicitor of others to lash out against the United States, go free because the government was also breaking the law? Meanwhile, al-Timimi remains in jail awaiting his appeal to the Supreme Court.

Domestic Spying and the Legal System

"The president ignores [the FISA court] at [his] peril," said Judge Harold A. Baker, a sitting judge in Illinois who also served on the FISA court, after it was disclosed that President Bush was ignoring the law that demands that FISA gain court approvals for NSA wiretaps.

Indeed, by ignoring existing law, the cases the administration have brought against individuals have less credibility. The 1978 FISA act gave secret wiretaps legal credibility because there was oversight by the FISA court. Without any oversight, however, who knows who is being spied upon, what information has been gathered, or for what use? The Bush administration has hardly helped its case, since it at first denied that the NSA program existed, then it refused to give Congress, the courts, and the general public any information about the program. Any inquiry into NSA activities by reporters gleaned little response other than to indicate that the program is classified.

The Right to Due Process

In an American court of law, however, that response is inadequate. In the United States, every citizen has a right to due process: to know what he or she is being accused of, who is accusing him or her, what evidence exists, and how it was acquired. The last two requirements of due process are undermined by the secrecy of the NSA program because any evidence acquired by the NSA, as well as the program itself, are classified. Put simply, no court would allow a case to proceed under such circumstances.

Judge Harry T. Edwards of the circuit court supported this argument in 2006, after hearing lawyers representing the administration and the Federal Communications Commission (FCC) defend their use of wiretaps. Judge Edwards said FCC lawyer Jacob Lewis's arguments were "gobbledygook."

Shari Steele, Electronic Frontier Foundation's executive director, and Kevin Bankston, staff attorney, are photographed at their office in San Francisco, California, on June 15, 2006.

The legal implications extend beyond government oversight and presidential powers, however. In 2006, an advocacy organization for citizens' digital rights, the Electronic Frontier Foundation, filed a class-action lawsuit against AT&T for giving the NSA "unfettered access to Americans' telephone and Internet communications." At just one of AT&T's data centers, in Kansas, electronic records of 1.92 trillion telephone calls over several decades exist. Can the NSA access those as well? The Fourth Amendment, protecting citizens against unwarranted search or seizure, is at stake in this case.

Moreover, hundreds of "enemy combatants" are currently imprisoned in Guantanamo Bay, Cuba; an unknown number of suspected terrorists are being held in foreign jails at the behest of the Bush administration; and dozens of American citizens are on trial for having ties to terrorists. Under the Geneva Convention and the U.S. Constitution, each and every American citizen deserves a speedy trial and due process. But if the administration has its way, many of the accused will never know what they are suspected of, what evidence exists, and how it was acquired. This not only limits the rights granted to the individual under the Constitution, but it weakens cases against those who do intend to bring injury to

Detainees in orange jumpsuits who are considered enemy combatants sit under the watchful eyes of military police at Camp X-Ray at Naval Base Guantanamo Bay, Cuba, in 2001.

Americans. As a result of the administration's unwillingness to acknowledge the NSA or explain to Congress and the courts about its workings, all cases that utilize

center for
constitutional
rights

Director of the Center for
Constitutional Rights Bill
Goodman speaks in New York
about a lawsuit the group filed
in 2006 against President Bush
and the National Security
Agency (NSA).

information illegally gathered by
the NSA remain in jeopardy.

Proposals for Reform

Understanding these implications, many people have called
on Congress to alter the original
1978 FISA to "accommodate"
post-9/11 national security risks.

One proposal, by Republican
senator Mike DeWine, offered
the administration the ability to
"eavesdrop without any authorization for 45 days," but the
officials would then need to seek
validation from either the FISA
court or a special congressional
panel. Democrats, and even
some fellow Republicans, have
balked at such flexibility, saying
that forty-five days was too long
to monitor anyone's communications without oversight and
approval. What everyone can agree on, however, is that
every communication being monitored must include an
overseas caller and at least one known member of a

terrorist group. Both Republicans and Democrats have universally condemned spying solely on Americans inside our borders.

Whether these proposals will lead to legislation or an overhaul of FISA remain in question, but the majority in Congress believe that the government should have court approval before spying on Americans. No one wants to relive Watergate or have the NSA illegally tapping communications and building files against people. Even ignoring the rights of "enemy combat-

Under the Geneva Convention and the U.S. Constitution, each and every American citizen deserves a speedy trial and due process.

ants" leaves people uneasy. Lincoln's suspending of habeas corpus has been compared to Bush's defying the Geneva Convention.

"Classified state secrets" is the defense the administration has been using, but with little success. The courts demand due process, and the sheer volume of suspected terrorists and those simply swept up in the NSA's "digital vacuum" programs forces greater clarity in the scope of the program. Thousands of cases still hang in the balance. The NSA program, and the Bush administration's legality in authorizing it, will most likely reach the Supreme Court, leaving Congress, American citizens, and many suspects in a legal limbo until then.

6
The Impact of Domestic Spying

Throughout history, presidents have expanded their executive powers, especially during times of conflict. Meanwhile, Congress and the courts have largely kept executive powers in check, maintaining a democracy. But just as the Watergate scandal brought about congressional hearings to rewrite rules about intelligence operations, so, too, is the possibility that the NSA program will be scrutinized by Congress. This debate has begun, and the 2006 congressional elections, as well as the presidential elections in

2008, will only increase this dialogue.

The legal consequences of the NSA program, however, remain unclear. Will alleged terrorists go free because the government used questionable tactics in monitoring their conversations? This point of contention has brought both political parties and the public together, united in the belief that fighting terrorists requires new rules, possibly even the overhaul of existing laws.

President Bush signs a renewal of the Patriot Act during a White House ceremony in March 2006, one day before it was set to expire.

Beyond the NSA, a greater debate has surfaced that questions the balance of power in a democratic government. The USA Patriot Acts I and II, legislation that was passed beginning in 2002 authorizing President Bush greater latitude to hunt for terrorists, have led to a backlash. Did Congress grant the president too much authority, which allowed for the creation of questionable programs? Oversight is critical; our Founding Fathers designed the government with a balance of power for good reason. Because they did not wish to live under a dictator, they created the three branches of government to work interdependently. In doing so, presidents were forced to work with the legislative and judicial branches to determine and enforce our nation's laws. Having the White House and both houses of Congress (the Senate and the House of Representatives) under the control of one party has only aided President Bush in expanding his influence.

"The Fourth Estate"

Even more critical is the role the press plays in overseeing government actions. It is the job of the press to inform the public, disclosing secret programs, political malfeasance, corrupt spending, and closed-door government activities.

"The Fourth Estate," as the press is called, is the independent watchdog over government. But even the press is under fire: multiple journalists have been subpoenaed for reporting classified information. Judith Miller of the *New York Times* was jailed in 2005 for nearly three months after refusing to disclose her confidential sources.

Once the *New York Times* broke the story about the NSA program, leading to a call for investigations, there were also calls for investigations into who "leaked" the story. Journalists must protect their sources—even if it means going to jail, as in the case of Miller. Former NSA employee Russell Tice has been threatened with arrest for being one of the *Times'* sources.

"As far as I'm concerned, as long as I don't say anything that's classified, I'm not worried," said Tice in

New York Times reporter Judith Miller walks into Federal Court in July 2006, followed by her attorney and the media to face criminal charges after refusing to disclose her sources.

a 2006 interview with ABC News. "We need to clean up the intelligence community. We've had abuses, and they need to be addressed."

Immediately, Tice's credibility was attacked. The NSA released information saying that his security clearance had been revoked in 2005, and that it had dismissed him based on "psychological concerns."

Under the Bush administration, this treatment is not unusual. Veteran CIA officer Mary O. McCarthy was fired in 2006 for allegedly revealing information to the press about secret CIA detention centers abroad. When she

Russell Tice, a former intelligence analyst for the National Security Agency, was fired in May 2005 after raising questions about a suspicious colleague while working at another agency.

stated that she knew nothing about CIA secret detention centers, she raised more suspicions about government activities. The CIA has consistently said that secret detention centers did not exist, but now it said that McCarthy had leaked information about them. McCarthy is suing the CIA for wrongly firing her. The outcome of her case remains to be decided, but the history of questionable intelligence gathering and the role the press plays in disclosing it remain controversial.

Room for Reform

Lessons can be learned on all sides from the NSA program. The government cannot act in total secrecy, the balance of power must be maintained, and the American people will not completely sacrifice their constitutional rights in exchange for security.

Given the ongoing debate, however, it is clear that Congress and President Bush are nearing an overhaul of NSA operations. Congressional leaders are demanding greater oversight, while the administration insists on confidentiality. The result will likely be a newer version of FISA that attempts to accommodate both sides. But since the NSA has already infringed upon the Fourth Amendment, will it be acknowledged under any revised version?

Perhaps the American people's only protection from increasingly losing rights is through the press and its continued publication of government threats of subpoenas and arrest. The day the press is intimidated by the government into not running a story, and whistleblowers believe they are not safe to speak out, is the day the Fourth Estate dies, and, along with it, democracy.

Domestic Spying and the Media

Some people believe that the discovery of the NSA program has become a scandal akin to Watergate, the Iran-Contra affair, and the more recent use or manipulation of intelligence to build a case to invade another country. However, the Bush administration would like to see its efforts defined in context with what it believes are the needs to protect the American people. Depending on your viewpoint, the creation of the NSA program is either an impeachable offense, or further instance of the president protecting the nation.

The debate over the NSA program includes issues that will never be fully settled: the balance of executive versus

THREAT OPERATIONS CENTER

NATIONAL SECURITY AGENCY

President Bush speaks with the press inside the National Security Agency on January 25, 2006, in advance of U.S. Senate hearings on his much-criticized domestic surveillance agenda.

congressional power, national security, and the activities of the intelligence community. Because the NSA program is entwined with so many other issues, it, too, may never be fully investigated, aired publicly, or ended. Although the press disclosed the existence of the program, the American people have yet to fully grasp its impact on their privacy and rights. The Fourth Amendment (protection from unwarranted search and seizure) has regrettably become a minor issue in the larger debate.

As divisive as the NSA program is, the sole means of affirming or rebuking the stances of politicians that support or denounce it is at the voting booth. President Bush won't be on the ballot in 2008, but his supporters will be. The Democrats will be as well, and their stances toward national security policies must also be weighed against individual privacy rights. Meanwhile, multiple court opinions either supporting or doubting the need for the NSA program have been heard as the cases continue to move forward to the Supreme Court, where the program's constitutionality will finally be fully considered, and hopefully, settled.

Instead of focusing on domestic spying and wiretapping, the debate over the NSA program should be focused on America's democratic values. The Constitution and the Bill of Rights have existed since the founding of the United States. Even under the threat of terrorism, should these rights be reinterpreted or sidestepped for our protection?

Will it take another failure in intelligence—perhaps another 9/11—to awaken Americans to the weaknesses of intelligence? By then, will the American public have any rights left to fully investigate? These questions will return to the minds of the American people and influence them at the voting booth, ultimately delivering the leadership and policy wishes of the majority of citizens.

Glossary

abet To encourage or support, usually of a wrongdoing.

abide To accept without question or opposition.

activist Vigorous support of a political cause.

adamant Unyielding in attitude or support.

appellate Having the authority to decide appeals, as in a court of law that deals with cases that have been appealed to a different court for another trial.

balk To hinder or stop.

behest A command or directive.

censure An official reprimand by a legislative body such as the U.S. Congress.

classified Information that is kept secret from the public.

COINTELPRO (Counter Intelligence Program) An FBI intelligence program started under J. Edgar Hoover to monitor dissident political organizations and activists in the United States.

decrypt To decode or decipher.

diabolical Especially wicked or cruel.

eavesdrop Secretly listening to another's conversation.

endorse To approve of or support.

felony A grave crime such as rape, murder, or burglary.

glean To learn, discover, or gather information.

implication Something that is suggested or inferred.

invaluable Something that is priceless.

jeopardize To expose to loss or injury or risk.

jihad In Islam, a vigorous crusade for an idea; sometimes mistaken for the phrase "holy war."

oversight An unintentional mistake.

pardon A release of wrongdoing by a high-ranking government official; forgiveness of a serious offense.

precedent Any legal decision that serves as a foundation for future cases.

probable Highly likely.

pundit A person who makes informed comments; an authority.

quagmire A situation that has reached a point where it is extremely difficult to resolve.

quell To suppress or stop.

retroactive Something such as a law or a pay raise that went into effect on a date that has already passed.

subsequent Occurring or coming in later or after.

subpoena A legal document that requests information, evidence, or the presence of a person to submit testimony before a judge in a court of law.

transgression To violate a law, court order, or demand.

tyrant A ruler who exercises absolute power; a dictator.

warrant A legal document that authorizes a police or federal officer to arrest a person, seize his or her property as evidence, or search a home or place of business.

For More Information

American Civil Liberties Union (ACLU)
125 Broad Street, 18th Floor
New York, NY 10004
(888) 567-ACLU
Web site: http://www.aclu.org

Electronic Privacy Information Center (EPIC)
1718 Connecticut Avenue NW, Suite 200
Washington, DC 20009
(202) 483-1140
Web site: http://www.epic.org

The Reporters Committee for Freedom of the Press
1815 N. Fort Myer Drive, Suite 900
Arlington, VA 22209
(703) 807-2100
Web site: http://www.rcfp.org

Web Sites

Due to the changing nature of Internet links, Rosen Publishing has developed an online list of Web sites related to the subject of this book. This site is updated regularly. Please use this link to access the list:

http://www.rosenlinks.com/in/dosp

For Further Reading

Bamford, James. *Body of Secrets: Anatomy of the Ultra-Secret National Security Agency*. New York, NY: Anchor, 2002.

Chesbro, Michael. *Privacy Handbook: Proven Countermeasures for Combating Threats to Privacy, Security, and Personal Freedom*. Boulder, CO: Paladin Press, 2002.

Friedman, Lawrence M. *Law in America: A Short History (Modern Library Chronicles)*. New York, NY: Random House, 2004.

Hyatt, Michael. *Invasion of Privacy: How to Protect Yourself in the Digital Age*. Washington, DC: Regnery Publishing, 2001.

Keefe, Patrick Radden. *Chatter: Dispatches from the Secret World of Global Eavesdropping*. New York, NY: Random House, 2005.

Wood, Neal. *Tyranny in America: Capitalism and National Decay*. New York, NY: Verso, 2004.

Bibliography

Lapham, Lewis H. "The Case for Impeachment." *Harper's*. March 2006, pp. 26–35.

Risen, James, and Lichtblau, Eric. "Bush Lets U.S. Spy on Callers Without Courts." *New York Times*. December 16, 2005.

Raw Story. "*New York Times* Admits It Held Domestic Spying Story for a Full Year" (http://rawstory.com/news/2005/New_York_Times_admits_it_held_1215.html).

Ross, Brian. "NSA Whistleblower Alleges Illegal Spying." ABC News. Retrieved April 20, 2006 (http://abcnews.go.com/WNT/Investigation/story?id=1491889).

Williams, Mark. "The Total Information Awareness Project Lives On." TechnologyReview.com. Retrieved April 20, 2006 (http://www.technologyreview.com/read_article.aspx?id=16741&ch=infotech).

Index

About the Author
Brad Lockwood is an award-winning author of several fiction and nonfiction books. His writings on politics, government policy, and public affairs also appear regularly in national magazines and newspapers. Lockwood lives in Brooklyn, NY.

Photo Credits
Cover (top left) © Prat Thierry/Corbis Sygma; cover (top right), pp. 3 (right), 31 (bottom) ©Tim Boyle/Getty Images; cover (bottom), p. 31 (middle) © Chip Somodevilla/Getty Images; pp. 3 (left), 4 (middle), 13 (top, bottom), 38 (bottom), 51, 53, 56 © Paul J. Richards/AFP/Getty Images; p. 4 (top) © Ron Sachs-Pool/ Getty Images; p. 4 (bottom) © Michael Springer/Getty Images; pp. 5, 44 (bottom) www.ourdocuments.gov/NARA; p. 7 Private Collection, Peter Newark American Pictures/The Bridgeman Art Library International; pp. 9, 39, 43, 46, 48 © AP/Wide World Photos; p. 13 (middle) ©Topical Press Agency/Getty Images; p. 16 © Hulton Archive/Getty Images; pp. 18, 23 © Bettmann/Corbis; p. 29 © Brooks Kraft/Corbis; p. 31 (top) © Joe Raedle/Getty Images; p. 33 © Luke Frazza/AFP/Getty Images; p. 34 © Kate Brooks/Corbis; p. 36 © Mandel Ngan/AFP/Getty Images; p. 38 (top) © Greg Mathieson/Mai/Mai/Time Life Pictures/Getty Images; p. 38 (middle) © Bilal Qabalan/AFP/Getty Images; pp. 44 (top), 47 © Petty Officer 1st class Shane T. McCoy/U.S. Navy/Getty Images; p. 50 (top) © Democracy Now!; p. 50 (middle) © Alex Wong/Getty Images; p. 50 (bottom) ©White House/Getty Images; p. 54 © Rick McKay/Cox Newspapers.

Designer: Thomas Forget; Editor: Joann Jovinelly
Photo Researcher: Amy Feinberg